CAREERS IN INFRASTRUCTURE

SOLAR POWER
Technicians

ADVANCED MANUFACTURING TECHNICIANS

AIRCRAFT MECHANICS

CIVIL ENGINEERING TECHNICIANS

ELECTRICIANS

ENVIRONMENTAL ENGINEERING TECHNICIANS

LOGISTICIANS

PLUMBERS, PIPEFITTERS, AND STEAMFITTERS

SOLAR POWER TECHNICIANS

TRUCK AND TRANSPORTATION DRIVERS

WIND TURBINE TECHNICIANS

CAREERS IN INFRASTRUCTURE

SOLAR POWER
Technicians

By Andrew Morkes

MC

MASON CREST
MIAMI

MASON CREST
PO Box 221876, Hollywood, FL 33022
(866) MCP-BOOK (toll-free) • www.masoncrest.com

Copyright © 2023 by Mason Crest, an imprint of National Highlights, Inc. All rights reserved. No part of this publication may be reproduced or transmitted in any form or by any means, electronic or mechanical, including photocopying, recording, taping, or any information storage and retrieval system, without permission in writing from the publisher.

Printed in the United States of America

First printing
9 8 7 6 5 4 3 2 1

Series ISBN: 978-1-4222-4666-5
Hardcover ISBN: 978-1-4222-4672-6
ebook ISBN: 978-1-4222-7148-3

Cataloging-in-Publication Data on file with the Library of Congress

Developed and Produced by National Highlights, Inc.
Editor: Andrew Morkes
Cover and Interior Design: Tara Raymo • CreativelyTara
Layout: Priceless Digital Media, LLC

Publisher's Note: Websites listed in this book were active at the time of publication. The publisher is not responsible for websites that have changed their address or discontinued operation since the date of publication. The publisher reviews and updates the websites each time the book is reprinted.

QR CODES AND LINKS TO THIRD-PARTY CONTENT

You may gain access to certain third-party content ("Third-Party Sites") by scanning and using the QR Codes that appear in this publication (the "QR Codes"). We do not operate or control in any respect any information, products, or services on such Third-Party Sites linked to by us via the QR Codes included in this publication, and we assume no responsibility for any materials you may access using the QR Codes. Your use of the QR Codes may be subject to terms, limitations, or restrictions set forth in the applicable terms of use or otherwise established by the owners of the Third-Party Sites. Our linking to such Third-Party Sites via the QR Codes does not imply an endorsement or sponsorship of such Third-Party Sites or the information, products, or services offered on or through the Third-Party Sites, nor does it imply an endorsement or sponsorship of this publication by the owners of such Third-Party Sites.

CONTENTS

Introduction 7
Chapter 1: What Do Solar Power Technicians Do? 13
Chapter 2: Terms of the Trade 28
Chapter 3: How to Become a Solar Power Technician 33
Chapter 4: Interviews 46
**Chapter 5: Exploring a Career as a
  Solar Power Technician** 51
Chapter 6: The Future of Solar Power and Careers 67
Further Reading and Internet Resources 74
Index 75
Credits 79
Author's Biography 80

KEY ICONS TO LOOK FOR:

Words to Understand: These words with their easy-to-understand definitions will increase the reader's understanding of the text while building vocabulary skills.

Sidebars: This boxed material within the main text allows readers to build knowledge, gain insights, explore possibilities, and broaden their perspectives by weaving together additional information to provide realistic and holistic perspectives.

Educational Videos: Readers can view videos by scanning our QR codes, providing them with additional educational content to supplement the text. Examples include news coverage, moments in history, speeches, iconic sports moments, and much more!

Text-Dependent Questions: These questions send the reader back to the text for more careful attention to the evidence presented there.

Research Projects: Readers are pointed toward areas of further inquiry connected to each chapter. Suggestions are provided for projects that encourage deeper research and analysis.

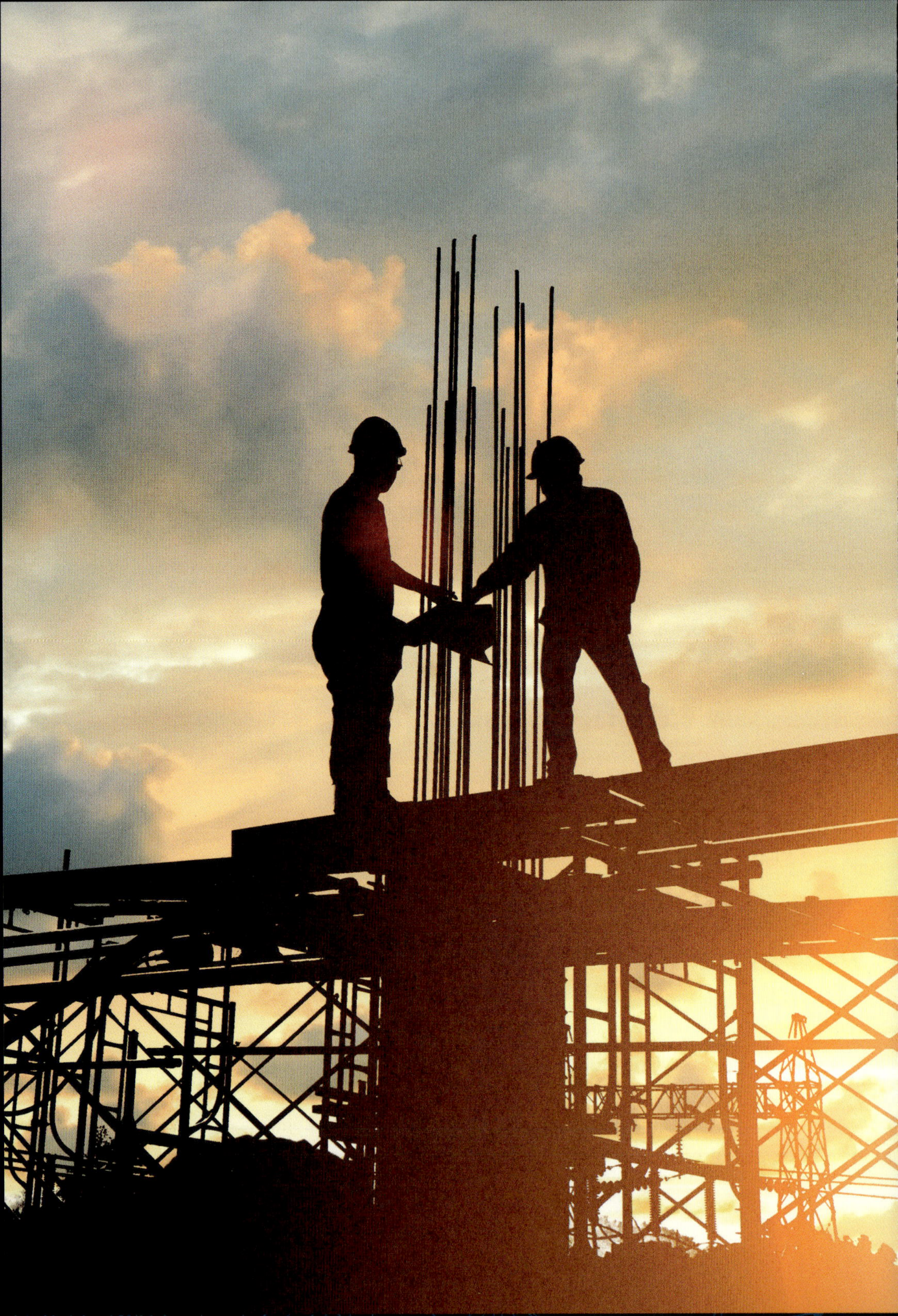

Introduction

Infrastructure careers provide a variety of good-paying opportunities that often have lower formal educational barriers than other occupations.

The word *infrastructure* might seem exotic to you, but did you know that you use infrastructure every day? Each time you take a drink of water, use your smartphone, turn on the heat or air-conditioning, or take a trip on a local street or highway, you are utilizing infrastructure.

There are actually two types of infrastructure. *Hard infrastructure* consists of all of the physical things (transportation, energy, water, telecommunications, and similar systems) that are necessary for the functioning of a safe and productive nation. *Soft infrastructure* refers to the educational system, law enforcement, emergency services, the health-care system, government agencies, and the financial system. These are needed to maintain the economic, physical, health, cultural, and social standards of a population. This series mainly focuses on hard infrastructure, but you will also see how hard and soft infrastructure work in tandem for the well-being of people.

Although infrastructure is very important to the success of any country, a considerable amount of the infrastructure in the United States and other countries is in fair, or even poor, shape. Every four years, the American Society of Civil Engineers publishes a *Report Card for America's Infrastructure*. It assigns letter grades based on the physical condition of US infrastructure, and the needed investments for improvement. Its 2021 report awarded a C- to the United States. If you received a C- in school, your parents might sigh and tell you to get back to work. And that's what the US federal government did (at least the work part), passing a whopping $1.2 trillion bill for funding to fix and/or expand roads, bridges, public transit systems, ports, waterways, and passenger and freight rail systems; expand broadband internet access; and help states and cities prepare for and respond to droughts, wildfires, climate change, and other environmental challenges.

Excellent demand exists for workers in many infrastructure careers. These are the people who fix roads, bridges, and ports, and build new ones; ensure that water is delivered to communities, and treat the wastewater created by people and businesses; build, maintain, and repair systems that distribute energy, and provide telecommunications services; move people in buses, trains, and planes; and perform a variety of other hands-on work. But infrastructure careers are not just for those who like to build or fix things, or transport goods and people. There are opportunities for construction and other types of managers; logistics professionals; building, bridge, and other types of inspectors; engineers and scientists; and workers in administrative, financial, human resources, and other supporting fields.

You probably already know someone who works in infrastructure. More than 17.2 million people (or more than one in every 10 workers) are employed in an infrastructure career in the United States, according to research from the Brookings Institution.

This is where you come in. The infrastructure industry needs you because there is a shortage of workers in many infrastructure careers. This has occurred for two main reasons:
1. In the United States, there has been a push for decades to encourage high school students to earn bachelor's degrees (go to college). It's a misconception that a college degree is the only path to a comfortable life.
2. A societal misconception exists, where people believe that workers in many infrastructure careers (excluding scientists, engineers, and managers) do not earn high incomes.

Let's take a look at both of these misconceptions, get the facts, and learn how careers in infrastructure are an excellent path to a comfortable middle-class life.

There are many quality careers (both inside and outside the infrastructure sector) that do not require a bachelor's degree or higher for entry. Many infrastructure professionals have associate degrees, postsecondary diplomas, or even high school diplomas. In fact, 53.4 percent of infrastructure workers have a high school diploma or less, according to the Brookings Institution. This is a much higher percentage than of workers in all jobs (31.7 percent) who only have a high school diploma.

Many infrastructure careers require training via an apprenticeship. An apprenticeship program is a great option because it provides both classroom and hands-on training to students. It also offers pay while you learn. As a new apprentice, you'll start out at a salary that is about 60 to 70 percent of what an experienced worker earns, and then get pay raises as you learn more and develop your skills and knowledge. Nothing beats earning while learning!

Some people who work in infrastructure obtained training by serving in the military. They were educated to be civil engineering technicians, plumbers, electricians, and workers in many other professions. Those who are in the military also receive a salary while they learn. After you leave the military, it is relatively easy to land a job. Many employers seek out former members of the military because they have a reputation for being disciplined, working hard, following instructions, and being diligent in their work. Some companies even have military-to-civilian worker programs to recruit veterans.

The second stereotype about many infrastructure careers is that they do not pay well. Again, this is untrue. There are low-paying jobs in any field, but the majority of infrastructure careers pay salaries that are equal to or higher than the average salary for all workers. For example, the median annual wage for all construction and extraction occupations is $48,610, according to the US Department of Labor (USDL). That salary is higher than the median annual wage ($41,950) for all careers. Median annual earnings for workers in installation, maintenance, and repair occupations are $48,750, which is also higher than the median annual wage for all careers.

In addition to good pay and less-demanding educational requirements (and options to earn while you learn), there are many other good reasons to consider pursuing a career in infrastructure. Some of those compelling grounds include the following:
- availability of jobs throughout the country, from large cities and suburbs to small towns and rural areas
- availability of a large number of jobs because the field is so large
- transferability of skill sets to different positions in infrastructure
- encouragement to enter the field by a growing number of programs and initiatives for women and people of color, groups that have traditionally been underrepresented in many infrastructure careers

In this book, you will learn everything you need to know about preparing for and understanding the career of solar power technician, from typical job duties and work environment to how to train for the field, methods of exploring the field while still in school, and the employment outlook. Finally, you'll get the chance to read interviews with solar power technicians and educators in the interview section of the book.

I hope that learning about the work of solar power technicians will inspire you to enter this field and learn more about infrastructure, and why it is so important to our daily lives. Good luck with your career exploration!

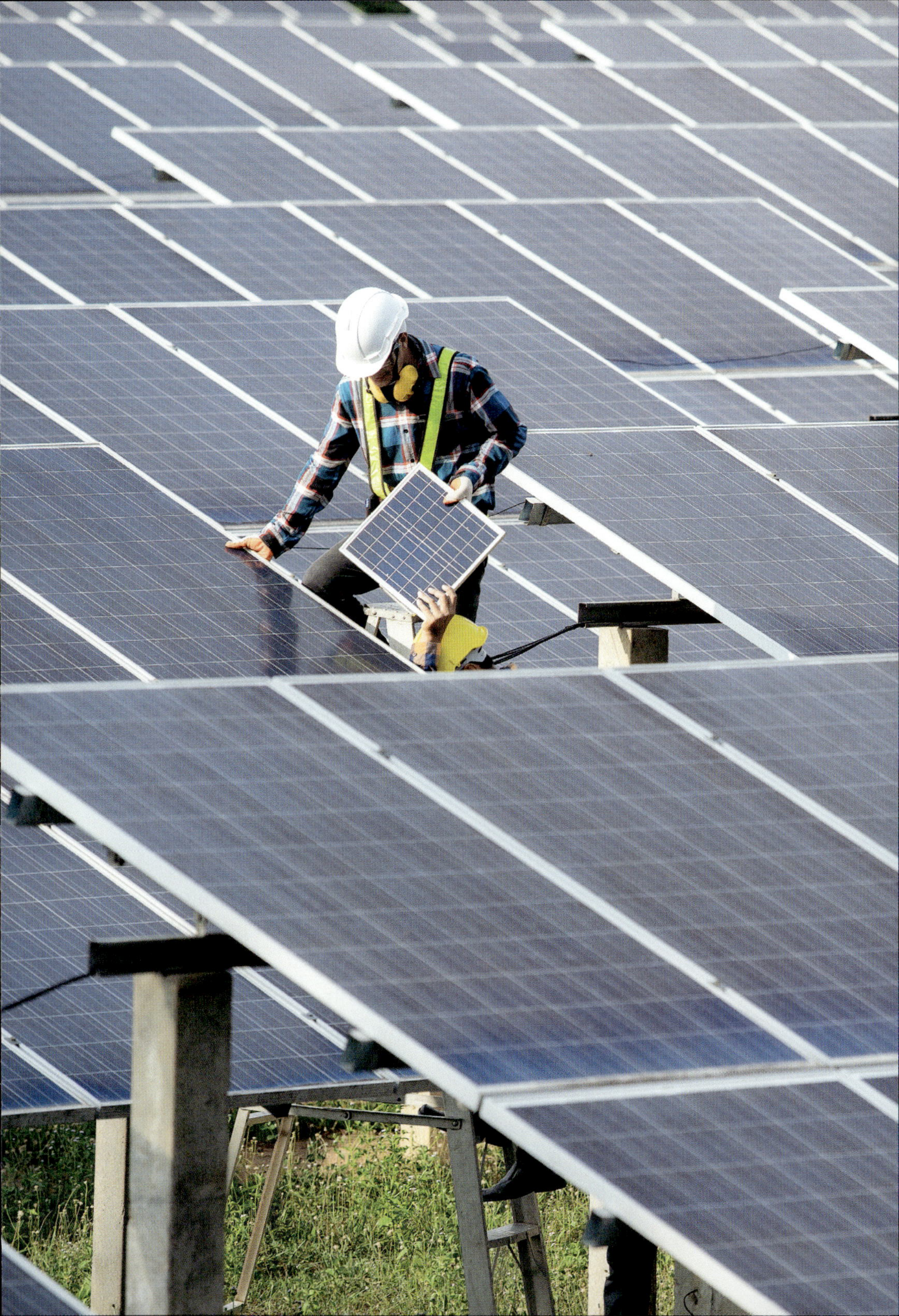

WORDS TO UNDERSTAND

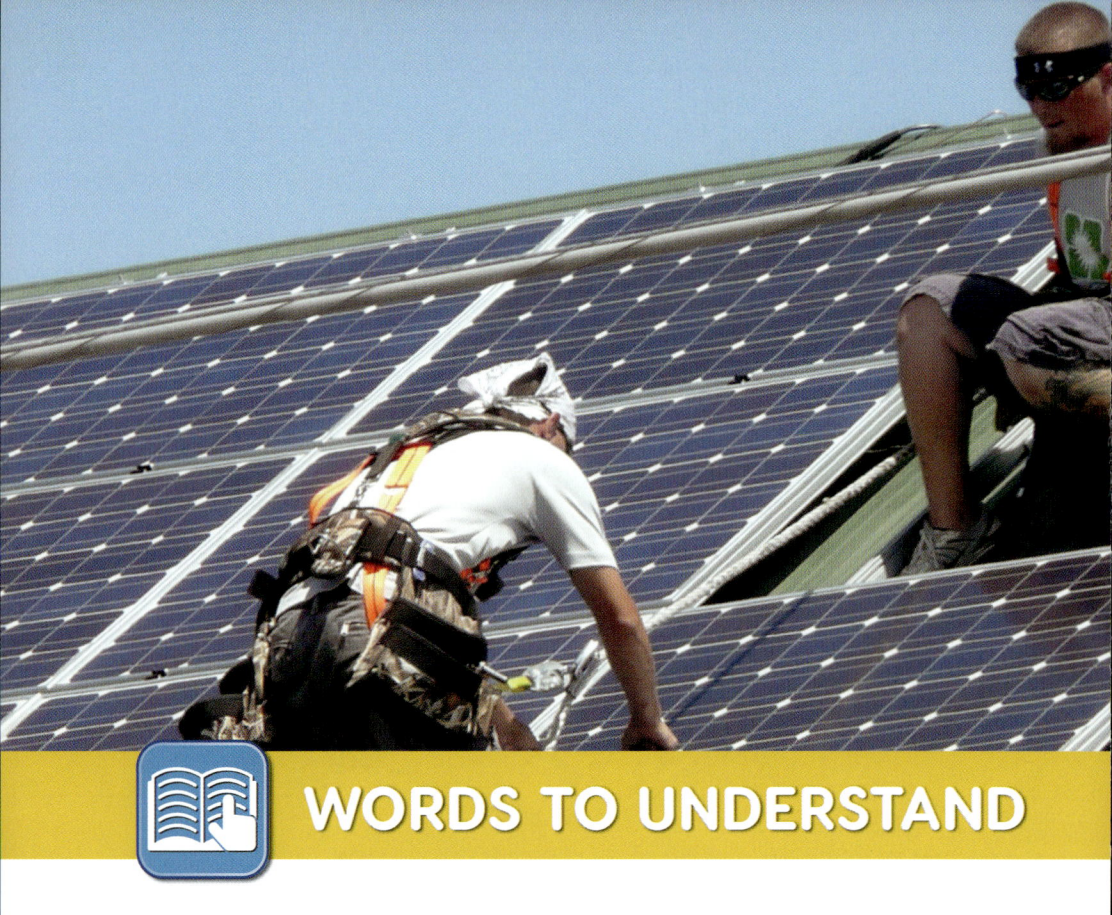

climate change: changes to the environment caused by both natural and human-created processes

combustion: a chemical process in which fuel reacts rapidly with oxygen and gives off heat

contractor: a person or company that is hired for a certain period of time to provide services, goods, equipment, materials, or staff in order to meet an established goal

electric grid: an interconnected group of electricity generators, high-power transmission wires, and lower-power distribution wires that connect electricity producers to end users

industry: a particular area of business, such as car manufacturing or hospitality

renewable energy: an energy source that can be replaced once it is used; the five main types of renewable energy are solar, wind, geothermal, hydropower, and bioenergy

Chapter 1

What Do Solar Power Technicians Do?

What Is Solar Power?

Solar power is energy that is produced by harvesting the heat and energy of the sun. It's a popular source of **renewable energy** in the United States, and in many other countries. Solar energy is popular because it is a constant, dependable source of energy. It is captured via several methods. Thermal collectors are used to capture solar energy and convert it to solar thermal energy to heat water for residential or business use. This captured solar energy is also converted into electricity. Solar-collecting power plants use the heat from the sun to heat fluids and turn them into steam. This steam creates **combustion** to power generators. Solar photovoltaic devices, or solar cells, convert the sun's energy directly into electricity. A small solar cell can power a small electrical device. Large groups of photovoltaic solar panels (known as solar farms) generate electricity for transmission to and distribution on the **electric grid**.

Solar power does have a few drawbacks. Solar energy is, of course, not available 24 hours a day, although it can be stored in batteries for use when no light is available. The amount of sunlight available varies based on location, time of day and year, and weather conditions. Additionally, the level of the sun's energy that reaches the earth's surface is quite small. As a result, large areas are needed to collect the energy of the sun and make it useful.

US ENERGY USE BY SOURCE

- Petroleum: 35 percent
- Natural Gas: 34 percent
- Renewable Energy: 12 percent
- Coal: 10 percent
- Nuclear Electric Power: 9 percent

Source: US Energy Information Administration

In 2020, renewable energy sources (including solar power) produced a record 21 percent of all the electricity generated in the United States, according to the Energy Information Administration.

Learn how solar energy works.

The Work of Solar Power Technicians

Solar power technicians build, install, maintain, and repair solar panel systems. Some connect arrays to the electric grid, while others install photovoltaic systems on the roofs of homes, businesses, and other buildings to provide renewable energy. Solar power technicians are also known as *solar photovoltaic technicians* and *solar power installers*.

Here are some of the main duties of solar power technicians:

- meeting with customers to determine their photovoltaic needs and assess site conditions
- identifying any electrical, environmental, and safety hazards associated with the planned installation
- measuring, cutting, and assembling the support structure for solar photovoltaic panels
- installing solar modules, panels, and support structures according to building codes and standards
- installing grounding systems, circuit conductors, and other components (note: electricians may handle these tasks in some work settings)

A technician records data at a solar farm.

Solar panels convert sunlight into electricity, even in below-freezing weather.

- connecting photovoltaic panels to the customer's electrical system
- activating and testing photovoltaic systems
- measuring and assessing system performance and operating parameters to determine if the system is working as designed
- conducting routine maintenance of photovoltaic technology, including modules, arrays, batteries, power conditioning equipment, safety systems, structural systems, and weather sealing
- repairing broken panels, faulty wiring, and other issues that stop photovoltaic systems from operating

Solar power technicians may connect solar panels to the electrical grid, although electricians may perform this task in some work settings. A residential solar power installer will often work with roofers to install solar panels. On larger installation projects, technicians may operate forklifts or front-end loaders.

Solar Power Technicians and Infrastructure

Solar power plays an important role in our nation's infrastructure because it replaces fossil fuels—such as coal, oil, and natural gas. These fuels create large amounts of pollution and other environmental damage during their extraction and use to generate energy. Using renewable energies, such as solar power, reduces the amount of greenhouse gas emissions (carbon dioxide, methane, ozone, etc.) that warm the earth's atmosphere and cause **climate change**.

In many states, the US electric grid and other energy infrastructure are aging and in need of significant technology upgrades to improve efficiency and reliability, especially in response to adverse weather events. For the first time, renewable energy (including solar)

IS A CAREER AS A SOLAR POWER TECHNICIAN RIGHT FOR ME?

Test your interest. How many of these statements do you agree with?

___ My favorite classes in school are science and shop.
___ I like to build and fix things.
___ I am curious about how things work.
___ I like to build electronics and other things that require electricity.
___ I am not afraid of heights.
___ I am good at math.
___ I care about protecting the environment.

If many of the statements above describe you, then you should consider a career in the field.

THE MOST USED TYPES OF RENEWABLE ENERGY

- Bioenergy: 39 percent
- Wind: 26 percent
- Hydroelectric: 22 percent
- Solar: 11 percent
- Geothermal: 2 percent

Source: US Energy Information Administration

accounted for the largest portion of new generating capacity in 2020, according to the US Energy Information Administration. Twenty-one percent of electricity generation came from renewable energy sources in 2020.

Follow a day in the life of a solar installer.

Since technicians often work on roofs, they must not be afraid of heights.

Rising demand for renewable energy in electricity generation will create a need for more solar power technicians. Additionally, these workers have a wide range of skills that make them good candidates to work in electricity generation jobs outside the solar **industry**.

Employers

Solar power technicians are employed by power companies; photovoltaic panel manufacturers; electrical **contractors** and other wiring installation contractors; plumbing, heating, and air-conditioning contractors; and power and communication line and related structures construction firms.

The top countries for solar employment (in descending order) are China, Japan, United States, India, Bangladesh, Vietnam, Malaysia, Brazil, Germany, and the Philippines, according to the International Renewable Energy Agency (IRENA). These countries are home to 87 percent of the solar workforce.

Technicians need excellent communication skills to work effectively as a member of a team.

What It's Like to Be a Solar Power Technician

Working as a solar power technician is a good career if you like a constantly changing job environment and working with your hands. Most of their duties are done outdoors, so technicians must be willing to work in a variety of weather conditions—from blazing sun to brisk and even cold days. Technicians do not work in dangerous or adverse

TOP STATES FOR SOLAR EMPLOYMENT

1. California
2. Florida
3. New York
4. Texas
5. Massachusetts
6. Arizona
7. Utah
8. Colorado
9. Ohio
10. Nevada

Source: *National Solar Jobs Census 2020* (published in May 2021)

conditions such as high winds, heavy snow, or rain. Technicians spend much of their time on rooftops, but also work in attics and crawl spaces to connect panels to the electrical grid. A solar power technician who builds solar farms works at ground level, although they may need to climb ladders or scaffolding to install or service solar panels.

Most solar power technicians work a standard 40-hour week, Monday through Friday, but some technicians work on weekends. Some jobs require a considerable amount of travel, and technicians who are constructing solar farms may work in remote locations that require long-term stays in hotels or other lodging.

This career can be dangerous. Technicians risk falls from roofs, lifts, and ladders; burns from hot equipment and materials; muscle strains from lifting heavy equipment; and shocks from electricity while installing and maintaining photovoltaic systems. As a result,

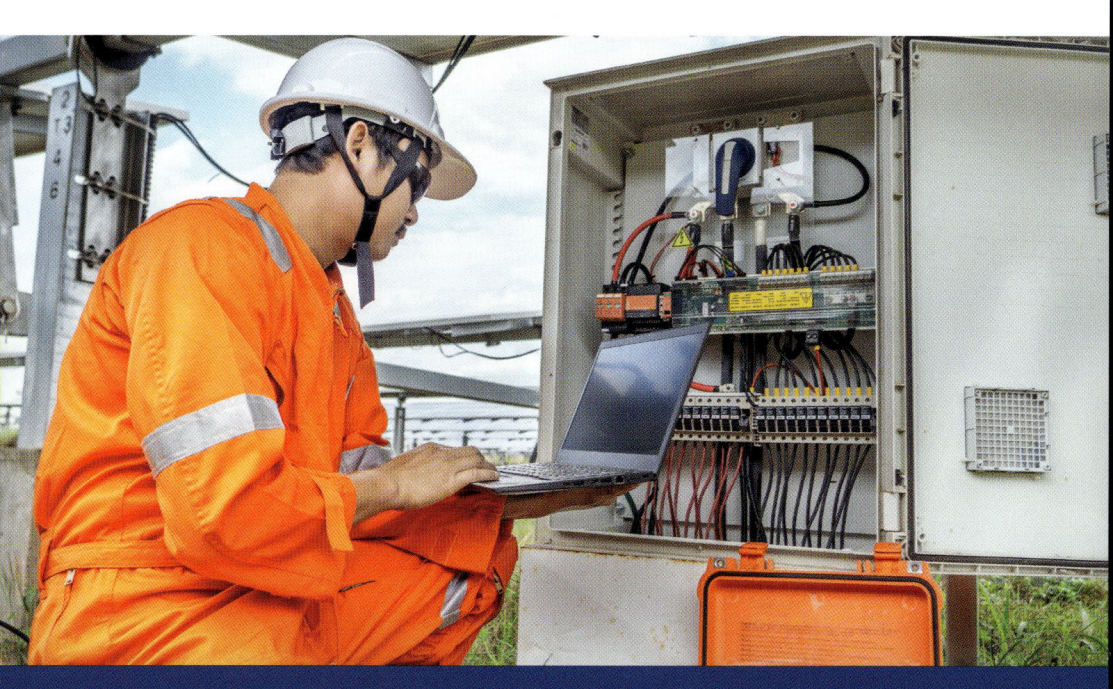

Solar power technicians must have a detail-oriented and analytical personality to identify and assess data, ensuring that solar systems are working properly.

they take safety very seriously. Safety harnesses keep them safe when climbing ladders and walking on steep roofs; hardhats, eyewear, boots, and gloves reduce the chance of injury; and strict rules are followed regarding the setup, use, and storage of tools, equipment, and construction materials.

Key Skills for Success

To be successful in this career, you'll need a combination of technical and soft skills. Technical skills include electrical knowledge, mathematical ability, proficiency at reading blueprints and schematic diagrams, and the ability to use tools and equipment. These skills are typically taught in college, in an apprenticeship, and during military training programs. Soft skills are personal abilities that help you to be successful on the job. For example, solar power technicians need strong communication skills (including listening skills) in order to effectively work with clients, coworkers, and managers. If you are

A supervisor (right) discusses solar panel upgrades with a technician.

DID YOU KNOW?

US News & World Report recently ranked the career of solar photovoltaic installer as the fourth-best construction industry career, and the 22nd highest-paying job that does not require a bachelor's degree. These statistics place installers in good company, because there are more than 500 types of jobs in the United States.

a poor communicator, you may misunderstand what the customer wants, or what your boss is telling you to do. These skills are also important because this career can be dangerous. It's critical that you communicate effectively with coworkers because you are working with electricity, at heights, and sometimes in confined spaces.

Strong organizational and time-management skills are necessary to do the job effectively and meet project deadlines. For example, if your tools and supplies are not organized, you might not be able to find what you need during a critical phase in the installation process.

A detail-oriented personality is important because solar power installation involves a variety of steps that must be taken in the correct order to build properly functioning systems.

Technicians need excellent problem-solving skills. They will have to address a variety of issues on the job, such as malfunctioning equipment, missing components, and unexpected structural challenges at the installation site.

Other important soft skills include the following:
- an analytical personality
- patience
- leadership ability
- creativity
- the ability to work alone, as well as a member of a team when necessary

Twenty-five percent of solar power technicians earn $55,760 or more annually, according to the USDL.

There are also some physical requirements that are needed for success in this career. Since technicians spend a lot of time on roofs, lifts, and ladders, you must not be afraid of heights. You should be in excellent physical health, and have stamina. You will be on your feet all day, going up and down ladders; bending, stooping, and reaching to install mechanical components; and lifting heavy equipment and materials. Solar panels can weigh up to 60 pounds (27.2 kilograms), and batteries can weigh as much as 120 pounds (54.4 kilograms).

Advancement

With experience, solar power technicians with recognized leadership ability can advance to supervisory and managerial positions. Some technicians use their extensive knowledge of solar technology to go into sales. Others choose to pursue advanced education to become solar engineers or college professors.

Earnings

Solar power technicians earn average salaries of $48,020, according to the USDL. Earnings range from $32,590–$64,600, or higher.

Earnings for solar power technicians vary based on one's geographic location, educational background, level of experience, and other factors. They also vary by employer. Here are the average salaries offered by major employers of solar power technicians:
- nonresidential building construction: $50,290
- utility system construction: $49,210
- electric power generation, transmission, and distribution: $48,850
- building equipment contractors: $48,560
- foundation, structure, and building exterior contractors: $44,610

Technicians who are members of unions typically earn higher salaries than nonunion members. A union is an organization that seeks to gain better wages, benefits, and working conditions for its members. It is also called a *labor union* or *trade union*. About 10.3 percent of solar workers are unionized, according to the *National Solar Jobs Census 2020* (which was published in May 2021).

CAREER LADDER

Solar Engineer or College Professor

Manager or Sales Professional

Experienced Solar Power Technician

Entry-Level Solar Power Technician

An electrician in the military (including those who build and repair solar systems) earns an average salary of $64,499. As members of the military, they also receive free room and board.

Solar power technicians who work full time (35–40 hours a week) for companies, government agencies, and other organizations often receive fringe benefits. These can include health insurance, paid vacation and sick days, and other perks.

SALARIES FOR SOLAR POWER TECHNICIANS BY US STATE

Earnings for solar power technicians vary by state based on demand and other factors. Here are the five states where employers pay the highest average salary and the states in which employers pay the lowest salaries.

Highest Average Salaries:
1. Oregon: $57,790
2. Texas: $52,210
3. New York: $50,920
4. Massachusetts: $50,850
5. New Jersey: $49,730

Lowest Average Salaries:
1. Tennessee: $33,930
2. Florida: $36,110
3. Ohio: $36,180
4. Maine: $40,300
5. North Carolina: $40,710

Source: US Department of Labor

TEXT-DEPENDENT QUESTIONS

1. What is solar energy?
2. What are three key soft skills for solar power technicians?
3. What is the average salary for solar power technicians?

RESEARCH PROJECT

Talk to two or three solar power technicians about their careers. Ask them what they like and dislike about their jobs, what a typical day on the job is like, what the necessary skills are for success, and questions about other topics that will help you to learn more about the field. Write a 500-word report that summarizes your findings and present the report to your shop class or renewable energy club.

Chapter 2

Terms of the Trade

active solar energy system: A system that uses mechanical means—collectors, pumps, and fans—to collect solar energy, such as in a solar hot water heater.

alternating current (AC): An electric charge that changes direction periodically. It is used to deliver power to houses and office buildings. Solar power must be converted from direct current (DC) to alternating current in order to be used.

antireflection coating: A thin layer of dielectric material that is applied to a solar cell to decrease the amount of light that is lost to reflection.

array: A collection of solar panels that are connected as a system in order to generate a target amount of electrical energy.

azimuth angle: A measurement used to determine the direction in which the solar panels should face, relative to the sun, in order to achieve optimal performance.

battery: An energy storage device that is used to save electricity generated by a solar electricity generating system. Both hybrid solar systems and off-grid systems use solar energy battery storage.

blueprint: A reproduction of a technical plan for the construction and placement of a solar panel or group of solar panels, as well as in the construction of a home or other structure. Blueprints are created by licensed architects.

carbon footprint: The amount of greenhouse gas emissions (carbon dioxide, methane, ozone, etc.) created by a person, product, organization, building, or event; greenhouse gases warm the earth's atmosphere and cause climate change.

climate change: Alterations to the environment caused by both natural and human-created processes. One major cause of climate change is the release of excess amounts of carbon dioxide from the burning of fossil fuels, such as oil and coal.

concentrating solar power: The process of using solar power to provide electricity for large power stations.

current: A measure of electrical flow. It is measured in amperes.

direct current (DC): An electric charge that only travels in one direction. Solar panels produce direct current. A solar inverter is used to convert direct current energy into alternating current energy so it can be used in the home or returned to the electric grid.

electric grid: An interconnected group of electricity generators, high-power transmission wires, and lower-power distribution wires that connect electricity producers to end users. Electric grids are used to distribute electricity to customers in a large area.

electrical conduit: A tube that is used to protect and direct electrical wiring. It is made of metal, plastic, fiber, or fired clay.

energy: Thermal (heat), light (radiant), kinetic (motion), electrical, chemical, nuclear, or gravitational force that is harnessed to perform the functions of life. There are two types of energy: stored (potential) energy and working (kinetic) energy. Energy can be further categorized as renewable (wind, solar, hydropower, etc.) and nonrenewable (coal, petroleum, etc.).

fossil fuels: Nonrenewable energy sources—coal, crude oil, and natural gas—that were formed millions of years ago in the earth by natural processes.

global warming: The heating of the earth that is caused by the release of heat-trapping gases (called greenhouse gases) as a result of burning fossil fuels and other activities. Greenhouse gases allow sunlight to enter the earth's atmosphere, but trap heat that typically radiates into space. The use of solar power and other types of renewable energy plays a major role in reducing greenhouse gas emissions.

hybrid solar energy system: A solar electric or photovoltaic system that is combined with wind power, other types of renewable energy, and sometimes even fossil fuels to generate electricity.

hydronic heating system: A heating system that uses hot water heated by a boiler. The boiler is fueled by solar energy or geothermal energy, and the heat is piped through tubes that run under floorboards, along baseboards, or through radiators.

nonrenewable energy: Forms of energy that cannot be replaced after use. These include coal, petroleum, and natural gas.

passive solar heating system: A heating system that captures solar energy without the use of collectors, pumps, and other devices. An example is a building that has large south-facing windows.

photovoltaic cell: Technology that absorbs photons of light and releases electrons, which are captured and used to create electricity. Also known as a *solar cell*. Photovoltaics are the basis for the operation of solar panels.

photovoltaic system: Technology that uses solar electric cells to generate electricity directly from sunlight via an electronic process.

renewable energy: Sources of energy that never run out and that typically have no or low environmental impact when they are used. The main types of renewable energy are solar, wind, hydropower, geothermal, and bioenergy. Also called *alternative energy*.

schematic diagram: An illustration of the components of a system that uses abstract, graphic symbols instead of realistic pictures or illustrations. Technicians refer to these diagrams as they build solar systems and farms.

secondary energy source: A type of energy—such as electricity—that is produced by using renewable or nonrenewable sources of energy.

solar cooling: The use of solar energy to power a cooling appliance.

solar farm: A collection of photovoltaic solar panels that generate electricity for transmission to and distribution on the electric grid.

solar heat for industrial processes: The process of using solar power to heat a process fluid and then transfer this heat to a supply system or production process in a factory or other industrial setting as hot water, steam, or airflow.

solar inverter: Technology that takes electricity from the solar energy system in direct current and uses it to create alternating current electricity.

solar panel: A single photovoltaic panel that is made up of solar cells connected together. The panel generates electricity via the absorption of the energy present in sunlight. Also called a *solar module* or a *photovoltaic panel* or *module*.

solar performance monitoring system: A monitoring system that is installed at a site where solar panels are located. It records how much electricity is being generated per hour, per day, or per year, as well as collects data to identify potential performance changes.

solar power: Energy that is produced by harvesting the heat and energy of the sun. Also known as *solar energy*.

solar racking system: Solar installation hardware that is attached to the roof. The solar panels are then mounted on this system. Racking systems can be angled for the optimal degree of sun exposure.

solar water heating: The process of using solar power to provide hot water for homes and businesses.

tracking array: A solar array that is capable of following the direction in which the sun moves in order to maximize the amount of solar radiation it receives.

WORDS TO UNDERSTAND

accredited: having been evaluated and approved by a governing body as providing excellent coursework, products, or services; quality college and university educational programs are accredited

community college: a private or public two-year college that awards certificates and associate degrees upon completion

National Electrical Code: a series of rules adopted in all 50 US states to be followed to result in safe electrical design, installation, and inspection; developed by the National Fire Protection Association

networking: the process of interacting with people in person and on the internet in order to get a job and learn more about a particular career or industry

professional association: an organization that is founded by a group of people who have the same career (technicians, electricians, engineers, scientists, etc.) or who work in the same industry specialty (renewable energy, health care, etc.)

technical college: a public or private college that offers two- or four-year programs in practical subjects, such as the trades, information technology, applied sciences, agriculture, and engineering

Chapter 3

How to Become a Solar Power Technician

Educational Paths

There are many ways to train to become a solar power technician. The minimum requirements to enter this field are a high school diploma and on-the-job training, but many technicians have certificates, diplomas, or associate degrees. Others prepare for the field by participating in an apprenticeship, while some receive electrical training in the military before transitioning to the civilian sector. Before we cover these educational paths in detail, let's discuss what you should do in high school to prepare for the field.

High School

A variety of high school classes will help you to prepare for a career as a solar power technician. Sign up for shop courses—especially those that teach you how to work with electricity and build things. Technicians use algebra, geometry, and trigonometry to calculate angles, areas, and measurements, so take as many mathematics classes in these specialties as possible. Taking English, speech, and writing courses will help you to develop your communication

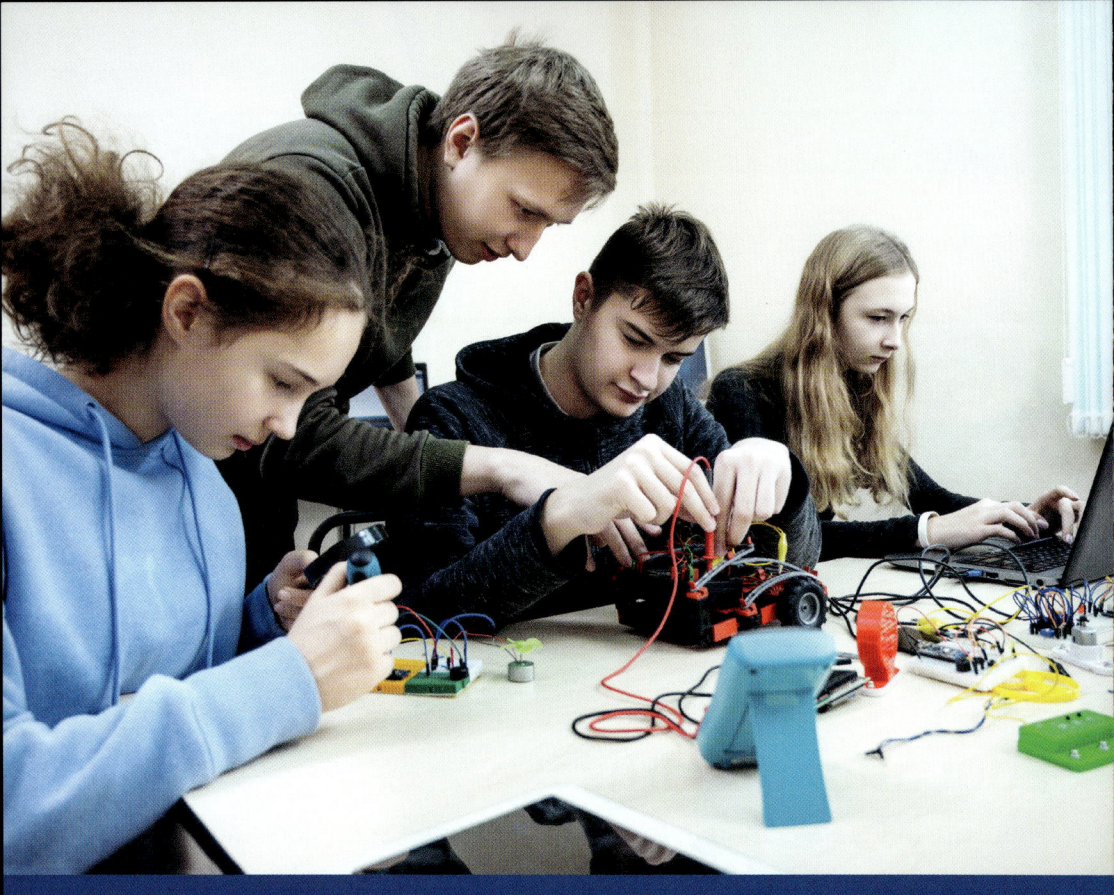

High school students build electrical systems that they will use to power a robotic vehicle.

skills, which you'll need to effectively interact with coworkers and customers, and prepare reports and communicate via email. Learning a foreign language such as Spanish will be useful because it increases your ability to communicate with people who do not speak English fluently, or at all. Other recommended classes include computer science, environmental science, and general science.

High school students who plan to enter the solar industry after graduation typically take a few solar power–related classes at **community colleges** or **technical colleges**, or that are offered by **professional associations** such as the Midwest Renewable Energy Association (MREA). Once hired, on-the-job training that can last up to a year is generally provided.

The electrical grid.

College Training

Many technicians have certificates, diplomas, or associate degrees in photovoltaic power, solar thermal technologies, renewable energy, sustainable energy, electrical systems/technology, or a related field. Here are some typical classes in a solar power associate's degree program.
- Applied Alternative and Renewable Energy
- Electrical Troubleshooting
- Electricity Basics
- Industrial Electricity
- Industrial Safety and Workplace Training
- Introduction to Solar Power
- **National Electrical Code**
- Programmable Controllers
- Residential Wiring
- Solar Array Installation
- Technical Math

Learn more about apprenticeship programs that are offered by the electrical training ALLIANCE.

Solar power.

An apprentice installs solar panels.

It's a good idea to attend an **accredited** program. The Technology Accreditation Commission of the Accreditation Board for Engineering and Technology is one well-known accrediting organization. It certifies schools in the United States and more than 40 other countries. Some nations have their own accrediting bodies.

As part of your college training, you'll also participate in a paid or unpaid internship. Interns work at companies that install or service solar panels, and receive on-the-job training that helps them to prepare for the field. Participating in an internship is a great way to explore a career, build your professional experience, and make **networking** contacts that could lead to a job. Your college will likely have established internship agreements with local employers. Additionally, some renewable energy associations offer such programs. For example, the Midwest Renewable Energy Association offers Solar Corps (www.midwestrenew.org/solarcorps), a workforce development project that includes an internship component.

Apprenticeships

An apprenticeship is a formal training program that combines supervised practical experience and classroom instruction. Apprentices receive a salary that increases as they obtain experience. By the end of the program, they earn as much as an entry-level technician.

Solar power technician apprenticeship programs typically last one to two years. Apprentices perform tasks such as loading/unloading equipment, assisting with general site preparation and cleanup, and installing conduit, wiring, and monitoring systems.

Apprenticeship programs are offered by the International Brotherhood of Electrical Workers (IBEW) and National Electrical Contractors Association (NECA) via local affiliate programs that use curricula created by the Associated Builders and Contractors, electrical training ALLIANCE, and Independent Electrical Contractors. Visit their websites for more information. Entry requirements vary by program, but here are typical requirements for those applying to an IBEW/NECA Joint Apprenticeship Training Program or an IBEW/NECA Area Wide Joint Apprenticeship Program:

- minimum age of 18
- high school education

THE SIX US MILITARY BRANCHES

- Air Force: www.airforce.com
- Army: www.goarmy.com
- Coast Guard: www.gocoastguard.com
- Marines: www.marines.com
- Navy: www.navy.com
- Space Force: www.spaceforce.com

- one year of high school algebra
- qualifying score on an aptitude test
- drug free

Apprenticeships are also provided by private solar power companies. Visit www.apprenticeship.gov/apprenticeship-job-finder to locate US-based apprenticeship training programs.

In addition, visit www.apprenticeship.gov for information on apprenticeship training programs in the United States. If you live in another country, contact your nation's department of employment to learn more.

Military

For the last decade or so, the US military has been working to convert many of its fossil fuel–powered systems, vehicles, and buildings to be powered by renewable energy (especially solar and wind power) or hybrid (renewable energy together with fossil fuel) systems. Why? To reduce energy costs, avoid potential energy supply disruptions, and promote clean energy generation and distribution. In addition, the branches of the US military need electricians—who also work with solar power in the military—to keep the power running at hospitals and office buildings, airplane hangars, and other facilities; install wiring in buildings under construction; and troubleshoot electrical problems. For these reasons, the armed forces

US Navy technicians complete the installation of a solar panel that will power a freshwater well in Chambok, Cambodia.

Becoming certified may result in an increase in pay, and it can also improve your chances of being considered for supervisory positions.

offer excellent training opportunities for people who are interested in becoming solar power technicians.

According to TodaysMilitary.com, job training for aspiring electricians in the US military branches "consists of classroom instruction, including practice in the installation and repair of electrical wiring systems. Further training occurs on the job and through advanced courses."

Some people enjoy their time in the military so much that they decide to make the armed forces their career. On the other hand, many people complete their service commitment and transition back to life as civilians. The skills that you learn in the military will allow you to easily find a job in the solar power industry. Some professional associations also provide assistance to members of the military who are transitioning to the civilian workforce. For example, the Interstate Renewable Energy Council offers the Solar Ready Vets program (which is funded by the US Department of Energy) to help veterans connect with training and jobs in the solar industry. Visit https://irecusa.org/vets to learn more.

A job applicant (right) shakes hands with an interviewer at the completion of a job interview.

Certification and Licensing

Certification is a credential awarded by a professional association or organization to workers who have met a set of established criterion (e.g., have a certain level of experience, have a certain degree, pass an examination). It should not be confused with an educational "certificate" that is awarded by colleges and universities, professional associations, and other organizations for completing two or more classes in a specific study area.

You do not need to become certified to become a solar power technician, but those who are certified often earn higher salaries and have better job prospects than those who are not certified. The North American Board of Certified Energy Practitioners offers more than five certification credentials for solar power professionals, including photovoltaic installation professional and photovoltaic installer specialist. Professional organizations for electricians and electrical/electronics technicians, such as the International Society of Certified Electronics Technicians, also provide certification programs.

Licensing is official permission granted by a government agency to a person in a particular field (engineering, nursing, etc.) to practice in their profession. In the United States, some states require solar power technicians to obtain a separate, specialized solar contractor's license. Licensing requirements typically involve meeting educational and experience requirements, and sometimes passing a test. Electricians, regardless of whether they work with solar power or not, must also be licensed.

RÉSUMÉS, COVER LETTERS, AND JOB INTERVIEWS

A *résumé* is a formal summary of one's educational and work experience that is submitted to a potential employer. Many employers request that job applicants submit their résumés online, or as email attachments, rather than in printed format.

A *cover letter* is a document sent with a résumé that provides additional information about your skills and experience. In recent years, some employers have stopped asking job applicants to submit cover letters, but this credential provides an excellent way to cover key information about your achievements, as well as convey your enthusiasm for the position that cannot be included on a résumé.

A *job interview* involves a formal discussion between an employer and a job candidate about their education, professional experience (if any), and skills. Such meetings are held in person, via the telephone, and via online communication platforms. Employers use job interviews to decide if you are right for a position.

Getting a Job

If you participate in an apprenticeship, or learn while serving in the military, you'll be placed in a job after you complete your training. But if you enter the field right after high school or after attending a community or technical college, you'll need to create a résumé and cover letter and begin looking for jobs. Here are a few ways to find a job as a solar power technician:

- Use the resources of your school's career center (high school) or career services office (college).
- Attend local job fairs.
- Contact companies directly about potential jobs; many companies allow you to apply for jobs at their websites.
- Join professional associations and participate in networking events, and search for jobs at their career websites (one good site is https://cleanpower-jobs.careerwebsite.com).

Finding a job may seem daunting, but it's just another life challenge to master. If you've worked hard in your training and have a positive, can-do attitude, you'll find a job in no time.

TEXT-DEPENDENT QUESTIONS

1. How do solar power technicians use mathematics in their work?
2. What are the minimum requirements to become an apprentice?
3. What is certification?

RESEARCH PROJECT

Talk to solar power technicians who trained for their careers in different ways (on-the-job training, apprenticeship, college, and military). Ask them what they liked and disliked about their training, and for advice on preparing for this training path. Which educational option seems like the best fit for you? Learn more about your favorite option(s). Write a 500-word report that summarizes what you learned and present this information to your shop class or environmental club.

Chapter 4

Interviews

Dr. Daniel Costin is an assistant professor and the chair of the Renewable Energy Department at Vermont Technical College in Randolph Center, Vermont. The school awards a bachelor of science (BS) in renewable energy.

Q. Can you tell me about your program?
A. The program in its current form was first offered in 2014, but its roots go back to a Sustainable Design and Technology degree program that was first offered in the 2007–2008 academic year. Renewable energy was an important part of that degree program, and it became a separate degree program in the 2014–2015 academic year. Students in this program learn to design and build renewable energy systems. Every class in the core of this program has a lab, where students do renewable system construction and testing. The main renewable systems are solar and wind, but the students also study energy efficiency and renewable energy heating systems. You can learn more about our program by visiting www.vtc.edu/program/renewable-energy.

Q. What part of your program do new students find most interesting and/or fun?
A. Based on our course evaluations, students enjoy using commercial software, such as HelioScope and HOMER, to do solar and other renewable energy design. We have a solar training roof on our campus, where the students learn safe construction techniques from an electrical and fall protection standpoint. We also have a small wind turbine and a full-size anemometer tower. Our renewable energy lab has equipment [needed for students] to study and work on renewable energy systems. Most students enjoy the combination of classwork and outdoor lab activities.

Q. Does your program offer internship opportunities?
A. All of our students have a summer work experience, which usually happens after their third year in the program. Many renewable energy companies and utilities in Vermont and surrounding states are happy to hire our students. A common job is to install solar energy systems ranging in size from residential to utility scale. Other students have worked on installation or assembly of energy storage systems. Our curriculum also covers efficiency and renewable energy heating and cooling, so some students have worked for mechanical contractors installing items such as solar thermal, cold-climate heat pumps, and geothermal systems.

Q. What is the employment outlook in solar power? How will the field change in the next five to 10 years?
A. The Renewable Energy Program trains students for careers in energy generation, energy distribution and storage, and energy efficiency. The latest report from the US Department of Energy predicts that annual job growth in these fields will be 7.0 percent, 6.2 percent, and 4.1 percent respectively in Vermont. Much of the work done in these fields involves transition of the energy system to renewable sources. In recent years, the energy storage business has taken off in Vermont, mainly using lithium-ion batteries. The industry needs our graduates, and we have a proven track record of graduate placement in these fields.

Josh LaBonte is the co-owner and director of field services at North Coast Power Systems (www.northcoastpowersystems.com) in Ohio.

Q. Can you tell me about your business?
A. Mine is a small business that primarily monitors, maintains, and repairs local wind turbines. We have also participated in a few solar projects over the years.

Q. What is the best way to train for a career as a solar power technician (SPT)?
A. As a student and a teacher, I found hands-on learning to be the most important factor to becoming a competent solar installer.

Q. What can young people do to learn more about the field?
A. I would do an internet search for relevant solar training [opportunities] and reach out to the teachers/directors with any specific questions that you have.

Q. What is the employment outlook for SPTs? How will technology change the field in the next five to 10 years?
A. The employment prospects and potential for the field change regularly due to the associated politics. There has been a fairly steady growth in the industry for the 13

years I have been involved in it, so I would assume always more jobs in the future as we continue to add to the total production from alternative energy sources. The technology is constantly improving to create more efficient and economically beneficial solar energy solutions. In five to 10 years, I see the technology continuing to improve and expand, reducing our carbon footprint and our dependence on fossil fuels.

Daniel Goodchild is the coordinator of the Construction/Renewable Energy Technology Program at Northwestern Michigan College in Traverse City, Michigan.

Q. Can you tell me about your program?
A. The program was originally offered as an AAS degree in 2012 or so. It has since been reformatted to be a certificate. The electrical emphasis, as well as renewable portions of the program, are offered at our Aero Park Laboratories building, a 25,000-square-foot open-bay facility with plenty of room to engage in hands-on learning. Visit www.nmc.edu/programs/academic-programs/renewable-energy-technology-electrical to learn more.

Q. What types of students enter your program?
A. The students entering the program currently are primarily interested in the electrical trades for a career, with a side experience in renewable energy. Many seek to become licensed electricians [to] have the opportunity to work on installation of solar photovoltaic systems.

Q. What personal qualities should students have to be successful in your program and in their postcollege careers?
A. All students entering any of the construction industry programs should have a great work ethic, like working with their hands and working outside at times, and be critical thinkers. As they enter the workforce, it will be additionally important to have good people skills, since much of the work requires knowledge of the customers' needs, as well as being able to describe the work in layman's terms to put the customer at ease.

Q. What is the employment outlook in solar power?
A. While the prediction for solar jobs is very positive, I have yet to actually see it taking off in the overall market. Residential solar would be the most dramatic demand for installers if the general public bought into it. This does not yet seem to be the case. While the cost of solar panels is about as low as it can get, consumers still seem hesitant in making the purchase. As it is, electricians are still more in demand

for traditional work than for installation of solar panels. I think people are still just not educated enough about solar panels to feel the initial investment is worth it.

Ramona Anand holds master of science degrees in both electrical engineering and in teaching and training technical professionals. She teaches at Lorain County Community College (LCCC) (www.lorainccc.edu) in Elyria, Ohio. She is founder and advisor of the Society of Women Engineers at LCCC. The college previously offered an associate degree in alternative energy program; that program is currently on hold.

Q. What are students surprised to learn about the field of solar power?
A. Students are surprised to know that the cleanest form of nonperishable energy is underutilized in many countries, including the United States. They are also fascinated by the scope of alternative energy.

Q. What personal qualities should students have to be successful in their education and careers?
A. This arena requires hard work, effort, dedication, and commitment toward education and meeting goals. Students also need to have an interest in plumbing, roofing, and other hands-on related tasks. In addition, good physical health is needed because installers must climb roofs for installations.

Q. What is the employment outlook for solar power technicians?
A. Solar installers are in demand, based on geographic need. Florida, California, Arizona, New Jersey, North Carolina, and a few other states have increased demand. However, there are some states where solar power is not [being] harnessed and utilized.

Q. How is the field changing?
A. The paradigm is shifting from the use of heavy panels to innovative material. Solar shingles are designed that can be installed in a couple of days instead of weeks—resulting in saved labor cost and increased durability. Accreditation agencies and the Occupational Safety and Health Administration [OSHA] are active in maintaining quality and standardizing the industry. Nonprofit organizations such as Green Energy Ohio (which is based in Columbus) are becoming more active. CREATE is a National Science Foundation–funded center that works in the field of alternative energy. It provides training to educators.

WORDS TO UNDERSTAND

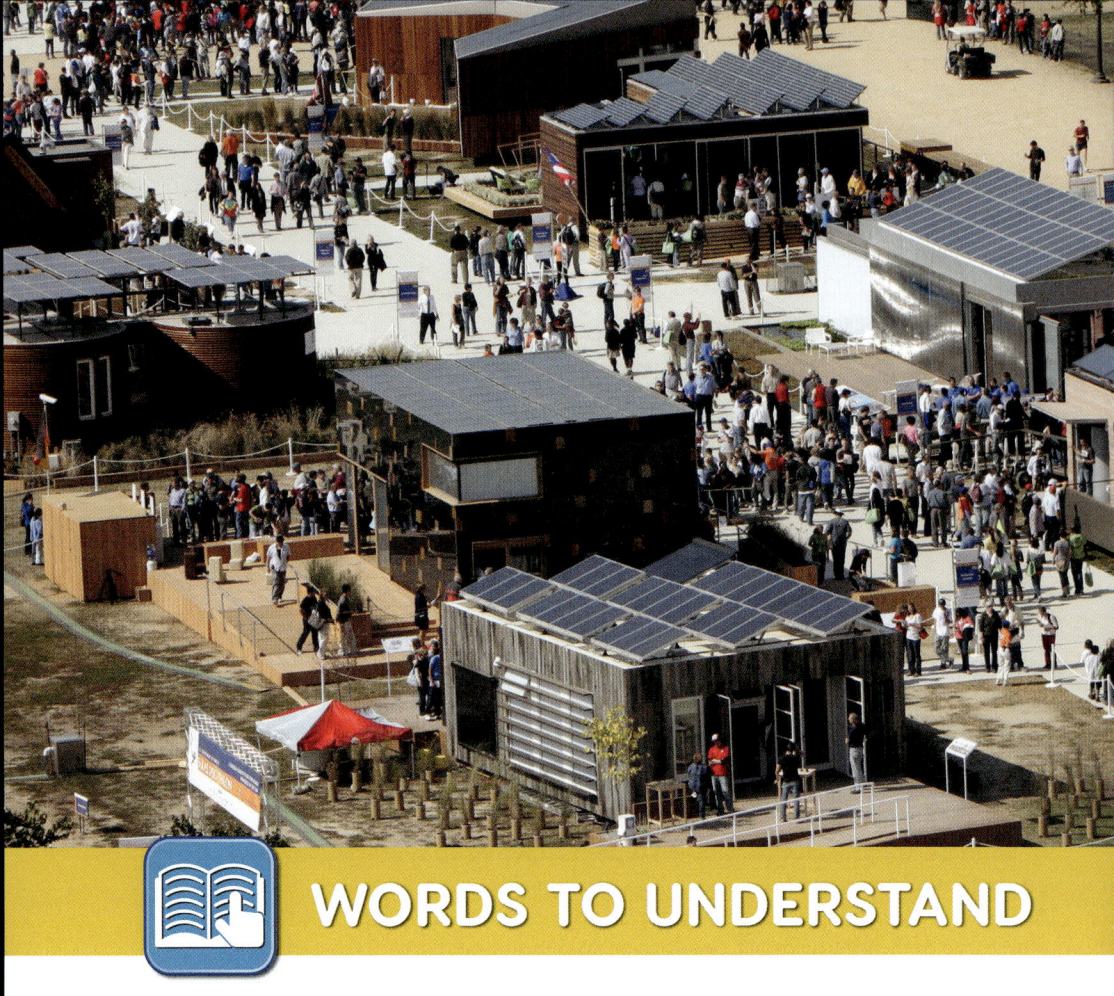

job shadowing: the process of following a worker around while they do their job with the goal of learning more about a particular career and building one's network

mentor: an experienced professional who provides advice to a student or inexperienced worker (mentee) regarding personal and career development

nonprofit organization: a group that uses any profits it generates to advance its stated goals (protecting the environment, helping the homeless, etc.); is not a corporation or other for-profit business

sustainable living: a way of life in which one seeks to reduce actions that damage the environment and find ways to reduce waste and energy use

Chapter 5

Exploring a Career as a Solar Power Technician

Learning More About Solar Power and Careers

There are many activities that you can participate in to learn more about solar power, and education and careers in the field. They range from something as simple as picking up a book or watching a YouTube video about solar power or the work of technicians to more active ventures, such as touring a solar farm or competing to build the best solar panel. Regardless of what you do, it's important to start exploring while you're still in middle school or high school so you can learn if a career as a solar power technician is for you. Perhaps your occupational explorations will lead you to conclude that you'd rather be a solar engineer, or sell solar panels to homeowners. It's better to make this discovery sooner rather than later, after you've enrolled in a solar technician training program. The following sections provide some great ideas on ways to explore the field.

Any experience that you can obtain working with electronics will be useful as you prepare for a career in solar power. Above, a high school student checks the wiring on a home computer.

Try Out Some Tools

Solar power technicians use a variety of hand and power tools to do their jobs. Examples include wire strippers, hole saws, hacksaws, pliers, cordless drills, nut drivers, conduit benders, torque wrenches, and crimping tools. You should begin experimenting with these and other tools so that you've at least had some experience when you start shop class or, eventually, begin an apprenticeship or other training. You might find some of these tools at home, at a hardware store, or at a local library (some have tool lending programs). Your shop teacher and parents can teach you how to use many of these tools (especially more dangerous power tools). YouTube is another good resource for tips.

Join the Technology Student Association (TSA)

If you're in middle school or high school and interested in science, technology, engineering, and mathematics (STEM), you should consider joining the TSA (www.tsaweb.org). TSA offers more than 70 competitions at its annual conference—including those in engineering design and technology problem-solving—and administers the Junior Solar Sprint, a competition for middle school students. It also provides opportunities to compete for college scholarships, develop your leadership skills, and help others through community service. Ask your science or shop teacher, or school counselor, if your school has a TSA chapter, and if not, ask them to start one.

Join an Association

There are many professional associations for current renewable energy workers. These organizations provide membership, networking opportunities, publications, job listings, educational offerings, and

A solar farm.

College students tour a combination solar/wind farm.

other resources to help workers develop in their careers. But did you know that some associations also offer membership options for high school and college students, and even those who just have an interest in renewable energy? For example, the Midwest Renewable Energy Association offers special membership categories for students, individuals, and families. Members receive free admission to the organization's annual Energy Fair, discounts on MREA courses, and other benefits. Visit www.midwestrenew.org/membership to learn more about membership perks.

    Another organization, Women of Renewable Industries and Sustainable Energy (WRISE), offers membership categories to college students and what it calls general supporters. Members receive access to networking and educational opportunities. In addition to the MREA and WRISE, contact state-level and local renewable energy organizations to learn about membership opportunities.

Take a Tour

One of the best ways to learn more about solar power is to view photovoltaic cells in person, and even entire solar farms. Many solar companies and associations offer tours to educate young people and potential customers about solar power technology. The American Solar Energy Society (ASES) National Solar Tour (www.nationalsolartour.org) is held each year, and it is the largest grassroots solar, renewable energy, and **sustainable living** event in the United States. In a recent year, it organized tours at more than 2,000 solar sites in 49 states, the District of Columbia, and Puerto Rico.

If you can't take an in-person tour, check out a virtual tour. The ASES National Solar Tour has a virtual component, and you can learn more about the science behind solar technology by participating in virtual tours offered by the National Renewable Energy Laboratory (NREL) (www.nrel.gov/about/education-students.html).

A solar racking system.

A coal-burning power plant. Coal is an example of a nonrenewable energy source.

FACTS ABOUT CAMPS

- Camps can last anywhere from one day to eight weeks or more.
- Some camps are free, while others require a program fee (scholarships are available at some camps).
- Most camps are offered in the summer, but some providers schedule them year-round on weekends and school vacations.
- Camps can be residential (you stay on campus in dorms or other comfortable buildings) or nonresidential (you return home each day after the session ends).

Participate in an Information Interview

An information interview is simply a conversation you have with someone in a particular career to learn more about their job duties, work environment, educational training, key skills for job success, and other topics. These interviews can be conducted in person, on the phone, via email, or through online video communication platforms. They typically last anywhere from 10 to 30 minutes, but you should let the information interviewee establish the ground rules regarding the length of the conversation and other interview parameters. An information interview is a great way to get information (obviously), but it's also an excellent method to build your professional network. The solar power technician you interview might be able to refer you to other technicians to talk with, serve as a **mentor** to you as you advance in your education and career, and even steer you to job leads once you complete your training. Here are some questions to ask during the interview:

- Why did you want to become a solar power technician?
- Can you tell me about a day in your life on the job?
- What's your work environment like?

- What types of tools and equipment do you use to do your job?
- What are the most challenging ones to use?
- What are the most important personal and professional qualities for people in your career?
- What do you like best and least about your job?
- What do you do to keep yourself safe on the job?
- What is the future employment outlook in your career?
- What can I do now to prepare for the field?
- What do you think is the best educational path to prepare for a career as a solar power technician?

Go to Camp

Summer camps in renewable energy, environmental science, engineering, mathematics, and other fields are offered by colleges, high schools, community organizations, museums, companies, and other providers. You can find camps by doing a keyword search on the internet and by asking your counselor and teachers for suggestions. Here are a few examples of well-known camps in the United States, and camps are also available in other countries.

4-H Renewable Energy Camp, Michigan State University
This camp—which is held in East Lansing, Michigan—is for young people ages 13–15 "with basic knowledge of electricity and who are interested in exploring the application, research, and opportunities in the field of solar energy." Campers tour laboratories and renewable energy companies, design and build a solar array model that they can use to provide power in their homes, and participate in other activities. Learn more: www.canr.msu.edu/4_h_renewable_energy_camp.

High School Renewable Energy Camp, Hamline University
At this camp, participants will design, test, construct, and build energy conversion and storage devices (such as solar cells, supercapacitors,

and lithium-ion batteries). Hamline University is located in Saint Paul, Minnesota. Learn more: www.hamline.edu/cla/physics/energycamp.

Various STEM Camps and Programs, National Renewable Energy Laboratory

The NREL is a national laboratory of the US Department of Energy that is located in Golden, Colorado. It offers a variety of in-person and virtual science, technology, engineering, and mathematics programs for middle school and high school students. Learn more: www.nrel.gov/about/education-students.html.

Join a Renewable Energy Club

Many high schools and colleges have renewable energy or environmental clubs that allow members with shared interests to learn more about these topics and make the world a more eco-friendly place. In such a club, you might do the following:

Learn what goes on in a renewable energy summer camp.

Middle school students participate in the LEGO MindStorm Robotics: Green Cities Challenge, during which they program LEGO robots to try to solve renewable energy challenges.

- learn about the tools and equipment that technicians and other renewable energy workers use daily
- build things, such as electrical circuits and solar panels
- visit solar farms to see how they work
- listen to presentations given by renewable energy workers
- organize and host an environmental career fair for students at your school

If your school doesn't have a club, start one! Ask your shop or environmental science teacher for assistance.

Participate in a Competition

Regional, national, and international associations; schools; corporations; and other organizations sponsor competitions for middle and high school students who are interested in renewable energy, electronics, technical, and related fields. Here are some popular competitions.

Junior Solar Sprint

In this competition, which is available in more than 30 states, middle school students work together to create the "fastest, most interesting and best crafted solar-vehicle possible." This competition is managed by the Technology Student Association for the US Army. Learn more: www.usaeop.com/program/jss.

SkillsUSA

This membership organization for middle school, high school, and college students who are interested in trade, technical, and skilled service occupations offers competitions in more than 100 fields. Students first compete locally, and winners advance to state and national levels. A small number of winners can even advance to compete against young people from more than 75 other countries at WorldSkills International. SkillsUSA offers several contests that will be of interest to aspiring solar power technicians, including Electrical Construction Wiring, Electronics Technology, Power Equipment Technology, and Related Technical Math. SkillsUSA works directly with high schools and colleges, so ask your school counselor or teacher if it is an option for you. Learn more: www.skillsusa.org.

Skills Compétences Canada

This **nonprofit organization** seeks to inspire Canadian teens to pursue careers in the skilled trades and technology sectors. Its National Competition allows young people to participate in more than 40 skilled trade and technology competitions, including Electronics, Computer-Aided Design, Welding, and Industrial Mechanic. Learn more: www.skillscompetencescanada.com.

Multiple Competitions, Technology Student Association

Middle school students can participate in the TSA's Electrical Applications Competition, in which they take a written test that evaluates their knowledge of basic electrical and electronic theory. Those who move on to the semifinals are tasked with building a specific circuit from a schematic diagram using a provided kit, making required electrical measurements, and explaining their methods to the judges. Another contest that is available for those with an interest in electricity and building things is TEAMS (Tests of Engineering Aptitude, Mathematics and Science), a one-day competition for students in middle and high school. Learn more: https://tsaweb.org.

Solar Decathlon

This collegiate competition seeks to prepare the "next generation of building professionals to design and build high-performance, low-carbon buildings powered by renewables." It is sponsored by the US Department of Energy. Learn more: www.solardecathlon.gov.

College students participate in the Solar Decathlon.

PROFESSIONAL ASSOCIATIONS AND ORGANIZATIONS

American Clean Power
(202) 383-2500
https://cleanpower.org

Canadian Renewable Energy Association
(800) 922-6932
https://renewablesassociation.ca

Energy Efficiency and Renewable Energy
US Department of Energy
(877) 337-3463
www.energy.gov/eere

Interstate Renewable Energy Council
(518) 621-7379
https://irecusa.org

Midwest Renewable Energy Association
info@midwestrenew.org
www.midwestrenew.org

National Renewable Energy Laboratory
(202) 488-2200
www.nrel.gov/research

US Energy Information Administration
(202) 586-8800
www.eia.gov/renewable

Wind Solar Alliance
https://windsolaralliance.org

Women of Renewable Industries and Sustainable Energy
(718) 260-9550
https://wrisenergy.org

Other Ways to Learn More About Renewable Energy and Careers

- Work on projects that use solar power to help poor or disadvantaged communities.
- Participate in energy fairs, such as the one offered by the Midwest Renewable Energy Association (www.theenergyfair.org).
- Read the Wind Solar Alliance's Wind & Solar Blog (https://windsolaralliance.org/blog).
- Land a summer job at a solar energy firm or another company or government agency that employs technicians.
- Attend open houses at community colleges and solar power apprenticeship programs.
- Participate in a **job-shadowing** experience with a solar power technician.
- Join the Boy Scouts or Girl Scouts and earn merit badges in Energy, Environmental Science, Electronics, Electricity, and other areas.
- Visit the websites of college and university solar power and renewable energy programs.
- Talk to your school counselor about career opportunities in renewable energy.

TEXT-DEPENDENT QUESTIONS

1. What types of resources are offered by the Technology Student Association?
2. What are three questions that you should ask during an information interview?
3. What is the Junior Solar Sprint?

RESEARCH PROJECT

Work with your friends or classmates to build a solar panel. Constructing a basic solar panel is easier than it looks, and many print and online resources are available to help you get started. Recommended resources include *DIY Solar Power: How to Power Everything from the Sun,* by Micah Toll, and "How To Build A Solar Panel From Scratch," by Kyle Wilson (https://thosesolarguys.com/how-to-build-a-solar-panel-from-scratch). You could also ask your shop teacher to create a lesson plan regarding this task so you can work on the project as a team, or do this activity at a renewable energy club meeting. Once you've completed the project, write a 500-word report that summarizes the process. What did you learn as you built the panel? What mistakes did you make that you'll avoid the next time you work on a similar project? Did you gain any insights about what it's like to work with tools and building supplies and the rewards and challenges of the work? If so, summarize these in your report.

WORDS TO UNDERSTAND

incentive: a financial or other type of award that is provided to a person or organization to encourage them to do something

robot: a self-controlled machine that is designed to perform tasks more efficiently and less expensively than can be done by humans, and to perform other functions; they are usually equipped with appendages that allow them to move and interact with their environment

tax credit: a tax incentive that allows qualifying taxpayers to deduct the amount of the credit (i.e., pay lower taxes) from the money that they owe the government for taxes

Chapter 6

The Future of Solar Power and Careers

A Bright Outlook

The US Department of Labor (USDL) predicts nothing but blue skies in regard to the employment outlook for solar power technicians from 2020 to 2030. Job opportunities in this field are expected to increase 52 percent during this time span, which is much faster than the average for all occupations. (Employment for all occupations is expected to grow only by 8 percent from 2020 to 2030.) The career of solar power technician is the second-fastest–growing occupation in the United States—after wind power technicians, where opportunities are expected to expand by 69 percent through 2030. Job growth varies by employment sector, but here is the employment outlook for solar power technicians through 2030 by sector:

- solar electric power generation: +112.0 percent
- plumbing, heating, and air-conditioning contractors: +68.2 percent
- specialty trade contractors: +60.9 percent
- electrical contractors and other wiring installation contractors: +59.3 percent
- construction: +52.1 percent
- foundation, structure, and building exterior contractors: +5.0 percent.

The use of solar panels in the residential sector is growing in popularity.

Demand for solar power is strong for a variety of reasons, which are detailed in the following paragraphs.

There is growing public and governmental concern about pollution and global climate changes caused by the mining, extraction, and burning of fossil fuels. The use of renewable energy sources, such as solar power, greatly reduces pollution and damage to the environment.

The cost of building solar farms and installing residential solar systems has declined significantly in the past two decades. In fact, "the cost of solar power has declined 80 percent since 2009 and 99 percent since the 1970s," according to the Wind Solar Alliance. This makes the use of solar power more cost-effective and more economically competitive with fossil fuels such as coal and natural gas. "New utility-scale solar energy projects are now often cost-competitive with new natural gas generation due to continuing technological innovation," according to the Wind Solar Alliance.

Solar leasing plans—in which homeowners rent systems, rather than buy—are also becoming popular. This trend will create additional demand because homeowners who rent will not have to pay the up-front costs of installation. The USDL says that "demand may be greatest in states and localities that provide **incentives** to reduce the cost of photovoltaic systems."

Major US companies such as Amazon, Target, Apple, and Walmart; government agencies at all levels; and the armed forces are taking major steps to utilize solar power in their buildings and equipment. They are also exploring other uses, which will create significant demand for technicians to install, maintain, and service these large and complicated systems.

The growing popularity of solar power in residential, business, and military settings will result in a strong need for technicians to maintain and repair solar panels, electrical systems, and related equipment.

The fossil fuel industry is getting in on the renewable energy revolution as well, which suggests solar power is here to stay. Many major energy companies are launching solar, wind, and other renewable energy branches to take advantage of the growing interest in clean energy. And companies such as ExxonMobil are utilizing solar technology on their oil exploration platforms.

DID YOU KNOW?

Eighty-nine percent of Americans who were surveyed by the Pew Research Center favor the construction of more solar farms. Only 9 percent of Americans oppose (were against) this type of solar construction.

Solar power trees are ground-mounted solar systems that offer an attractive and useful alternative to traditional solar installations. Seating and other features can be installed below the "tree."

Good Demand in Canada

Job opportunities for solar power technicians in Canada should be good during the next decade, especially in utility-scale solar installations. "This sector of the industry is poised for significant growth," according to the Canadian Renewable Energy Association, "driven by massive cost reductions and the need for nongreenhouse-gas–emitting electricity generation to address climate change." The government of Canada says that employment for solar panel installers will be best in Nova Scotia and on Prince Edward Island.

Opportunities in Other Countries

Demand for solar power will be strong throughout the world because it is a clean and renewable source of energy. Using more solar power will help many countries (such as China) meet greenhouse-emission–reduction goals. The top five countries using solar energy are China (which has nearly three times the solar capacity of the US), United States, Japan, Germany, and India.

About 3.8 million people work in the solar photovoltaic sector worldwide, according to the International Renewable Energy Agency (IRENA), which says that "growing shares of those jobs are off-grid (in regard to the solar industry, not connected to the electrical grid), supporting productive use in farming, food processing and healthcare in previously remote, isolated, energy-poor communities." Solar and wind power are expected to generate 50 percent of electricity in the world by 2050, according to Bloomberg New Energy Finance, a leading provider of strategic research.

Factors That Could Slow Employment Growth

Demand for solar power may decrease if the price of fossil fuel exploration, extraction, and usage declines, or if scientists discover better ways to reduce or eliminate pollution caused by the burning of these fuels. This is unlikely to happen because many fossil fuels (especially oil) are located in hard-to-reach or environmentally

DID YOU KNOW?

Thirty-three percent of the global renewable energy workforce is employed in the solar power sector. Sixty-three percent of all renewable energy jobs are found in Asian countries.

Source: IRENA

sensitive areas that are avoided by energy companies. Additionally, while scientists have developed ways to reduce pollution in some fossil fuel production, extraction, and burning processes, large amounts of pollution and environmental damage are still being caused by the use of fossil fuels. Renewable energy provides a cost-effective and environmentally safer alternate to the use of oil, coal, and natural gas.

Adoption of solar power may slow if the cost to manufacture and install solar systems increases. But the rapid adoption of solar power by the public, corporations, and the government (including the military) has fueled declining prices for this technology.

Many governments provide substantial **tax credits** to consumers who install photovoltaic technology in their homes or businesses. Those who install solar technology can receive a tax credit for a percentage of the cost of a solar photovoltaic system and other associated expenses. If these tax credits are eliminated, fewer people may install photovoltaic technology, which would reduce demand for technicians.

Robots may be developed that replace the work of technicians. But no such technology exists today, and any "technician robots" that are introduced will likely be used to perform low-level tasks (such as carrying and lifting equipment and materials) and augment the work of technicians, rather than replace them.

Finally, job opportunities for technicians may slow if too many people enter this career. This is a reality for any occupational field. The best way to prepare for this possibility is to make yourself an appealing job candidate by earning an associate's degree and in-demand industry certifications, as well as obtaining extensive experience in both residential and utility-scale installations. Additionally, those who are willing to travel to work in areas where demand is higher will have the best job prospects.

TEXT-DEPENDENT QUESTIONS

1. What is the employment outlook for technicians in the US through 2030?
2. Why is demand strong for solar power?
3. Which country is the largest user of solar power?

RESEARCH PROJECT

Talk to three technicians about the future of solar power installation, maintenance, and repair. Ask them how they think the field will change, what emerging technologies will be integrated into the field, and how skill and training requirements may change in the next decade. Incorporate their feedback into your educational and career planning, and write a 250-word report that summarizes your findings. Present the report at a renewable energy career fair or to your environment club.

FURTHER READING

Mayfield, Ryan. *Photovoltaic Design & Installation For Dummies.* Hoboken, NJ: For Dummies, 2019.

Patel, Mukund R., and Omid Beik. *Wind and Solar Power Systems: Design, Analysis, and Operation.* 3rd ed. Boca Raton, FL: CRC Press, 2021.

Peake, Stephen. *Renewable Energy: Ten Short Lessons.* Baltimore, MD: Johns Hopkins University Press, 2021.

Usher, Bruce. *Renewable Energy: A Primer for the Twenty-First Century.* New York: Columbia University Press, 2019.

INTERNET RESOURCES

www.nrel.gov/research/learning.html: This website from the National Renewable Energy Laboratory is a great place to start to learn about the various types of renewable energy—from solar, wind, and bioenergy to geothermal, hydrogen, and advanced vehicles and fuels.

www.bls.gov/ooh/construction-and-extraction/solar-photovoltaic-installers.htm: This section of the *Occupational Outlook Handbook* features information on job duties, educational requirements, salaries, and the employment outlook for solar photovoltaic installers.

www.onetonline.org: This US government website offers information on job duties, required skills, educational requirements, and other information for solar photovoltaic installers, solar thermal installers and technicians, solar energy systems engineers, solar sales representatives and assessors, and solar energy installation managers.

www.energy.gov/eere/solar/solar-energy-careers: The US Department of Energy offers a Solar Career Map that allows users to explore 40 jobs across four industry sectors and identify more than 60 paths to advancement between them.

INDEX

A
Accreditation Board for Engineering and Technology, 38
accredited programs, 32, 38
Air Force, 39
Amazon, 69
American Clean Power, 63
American Society of Civil Engineers, 7
American Solar Energy Society (ASES) National Solar Tour, 55
Anand, Ramona, 49
Apple, 69
apprenticeships
    discussion, 9, 36, 44–45
    education, 39–40, 52, 64
Army, 39, 61
ASES (American Solar Energy Society) National Solar Tour, 55
Associated Builders and Contractors, 39
associate's degree, 9, 33, 36, 49, 72

B
bachelor's degree, 8–9, 23
Beik, Omid, 74
bioenergy, 12, 18, 30, 74
Bloomberg New Energy Finance, 71
blueprints, 22, 28
Boy Scouts, 64
Brookings Institution, 8–9

C
camps, 58–59
Canada, 61, 70
Canadian Renewable Energy Association, 63, 70
carbon footprint, 29, 48
careers. *See also* jobs
    career ladder, 25
    in infrastructure, 7–10, 12
    as solar power technicians, 17, 20–22
certification, 41–43
China, 19, 71
climate change, 12, 17, 29, 68, 70
clubs, 59–60
coal
    discussion, 14, 17, 29–30, 56
    future of, 68, 72

Coast Guard, 39
college
    community, 32, 34, 64
    discussion, 36, 38
    professors, 24–25
    programs, 46–49
competitions, 60–62
Construction/Renewable Energy Technology Program, 48–49
contractors, 12, 19, 25, 43, 67
Costin, Daniel, 46–47
cover letter, 43–44
CREATE, 49

D
DIY Solar Power (Toll), 65

E
education
    apprenticeships, 39–40
    camps, 58–59
    career services office, 44
    certification, 41–43
    college and university, 36, 38, 46–49
    competitions, 60–62
    counselors, 53, 61, 64
    discussion, 33, 51, 64
    high school, 33–34
    information interviews, 57–58
    internships, 38, 47
    licensing, 43
    military, 40–41
    professional associations, 53–54
    renewable energy clubs, 59–60
    scholarships, 53, 57
    summer camps, 58–59
    taking a tour, 54–55
    Technology Student Association, 53
    trying out some tools, 52
electric grid
    discussion, 12–13, 17, 29, 35
    and technicians, 15–16, 21
Electrical Applications Competition, 61–62
electrical training ALLIANCE, 36, 39
electricians
    discussion, 15–16, 43, 48–49
    military, 9, 26, 40–41

INDEX

employers, 19, 25
Energy Efficiency and Renewable Energy, 63
energy fairs, 54
entry-level solar power technician, 25, 39
experienced solar power technician, 25
ExxonMobil, 69

F
fossil fuels
 discussion, 17, 29–30, 40, 48
 future of, 68–69, 71–72
4-H Renewable Energy Camp, 58

G
geothermal power, 12, 18, 30, 47, 74
Germany, 19, 71
Girl Scouts, 64
global warming, 30
Goodchild, Daniel, 48–49
Green Energy-Ohio, 49
greenhouse gas emissions, 17, 29–30, 70–71

H
Hamline University, 58–59
hard infrastructure, 7
heating systems, 30–31
heights, fear of, 17, 19, 24
high school, 33–34
High School Renewable Energy Camp, 58–59
"How To Build A Solar Panel From Scratch" (Wilson), 65
hydropower, 12, 18, 29–30

I
IBEW (International Brotherhood of Electrical Workers), 39
Independent Electrical Contractors, 39
India, 19, 71
information interviews, 57–58
infrastructure
 discussion, 7–10, 12
 and solar power technicians, 17–19
inspectors, 8
International Brotherhood of Electrical Workers (IBEW), 39
International Renewable Energy Agency (IRENA), 19, 71
International Society of Certified Electronics Technicians, 43
internships, 38, 47
Interstate Renewable Energy Council, 41, 63
interviews
 college programs, 46–49
 information, 57–58
 job, 42–43
IRENA (International Renewable Energy Agency), 19, 71

J
Japan, 19, 71
jobs
 in infrastructure, 7–10, 12
 job fairs, 44
 job interviews, 42–43
 job shadowing, 50, 64
 as solar power technicians, 17, 20–22
Junior Solar Sprint, 53, 61

L
LaBonte, Josh, 47–48
LEGO MindStorm Robotics: Green Cities Challenge, 60
licensing, 43
Lorain County Community College, 49

M
managers, 8, 22, 25
Marines, 39
Mayfield, Ryan, 74
mentors, 50, 57
Michigan State University, 58
Midwest Renewable Energy Association (MREA), 34, 38, 54, 63–64
military
 discussion, 9, 26, 39, 44, 69
 education, 40–41

N
National Electrical Code, 32, 36
National Electrical Contractors Association (NECA), 39
National Renewable Energy Laboratory (NREL), 55, 59, 63, 74
National Solar Jobs Census 2020, 20, 25

natural gas
  discussion, 14, 17, 29–30
  future of, 68, 72
Navy, 39–40
NECA (National Electrical Contractors Association), 39
networking, 32, 38, 44, 53–54
nonprofit organizations, 49–50, 61
nonrenewable energy, 29–30, 56
North American Board of Certified Energy Practitioners, 42
North Coast Power Systems, 47–48
Northwestern Michigan College, 48–49
NREL (National Renewable Energy Laboratory), 55, 59, 63, 74
nuclear electric power, 14

O
Occupational Safety and Health Administration (OSHA), 49
off-grid, 28, 66, 71
oil, 17, 29, 69, 71–72

P
Patel, Mukund R., 74
Peake, Stephen, 74
petroleum, 14, 29–30
Photovoltaic Design & Installation For Dummies (Mayfield), 74
photovoltaic systems
  discussion, 30
  future of, 69, 72
  installation of, 15–16, 21, 48
professional associations
  discussion, 32, 41–44
  and education, 53–54
  list of, 63

Q
QR videos
  apprenticeship programs, 36
  how solar energy works, 14
  renewable energy summer camps, 59
  solar installers, 18

R
renewable energy. *See also* solar power
  camps, 58–59
  clubs, 59–60
  college programs, 46–48
  discussion, 12, 30, 36, 40, 64
  future of, 68–69, 71–72
  professional associations, 38, 54, 63
  types of, 18
  use in USA, 14, 17–18
Renewable Energy: A Primer for the Twenty-First Century (Usher), 74
Renewable Energy Program, 46–47
Renewable Energy: Ten Short Lessons (Peake), 74
research projects
  building a solar panel, 65
  educational options, 45
  future of solar power, 73
  interviewing solar power technicians, 27
résumé, 43–44
robots, 60, 66, 72

S
safety, 21–23
salaries, 9, 24–26
sales professionals, 25
scholarships, 53, 57
skills, 20–24
Skills Compétences Canada, 61
SkillsUSA, 61
soft infrastructure, 7
soft skills, 22–23
Solar Career Map, 74
solar cells, 13, 30–31, 58
Solar Corps, 38
Solar Decathlon, 62
solar engineers, 24–25, 51
solar farms
  discussion, 13, 15, 21, 31, 53
  future of, 68–69
  visiting of, 55, 60
solar heating systems, 30–31

INDEX

solar installers. *See also* solar power technicians
    discussion, 15–16, 18, 23, 70
    education, 42, 47–49
solar leasing plans, 69
solar panels
    cost of, 48–49
    discussion, 13, 16, 24, 31, 65
    and education, 51, 60
    future of, 68–69
    installation of, 21–22, 38, 40
solar photovoltaic technicians. *See* solar power technicians
solar power
    discussion, 13–14, 18, 31
    future of, 67–69, 71–72
    opportunities in other countries, 70–71
    QR video, 14
solar power technicians
    discussion, 24
    duties of, 15–16
    employers of, 19, 25
    future of, 67–69, 71–72
    and infrastructure, 17–19
    job search strategies, 44
    opportunities in other countries, 70–71
    salaries, 24–26
    skills, 20–24
    work environment, 20–22
solar power trees, 70
solar racking system, 31, 55
Solar Ready Vets program, 41
summer camps, 58–59

T
Target, 69
tax credits, 66, 72
TEAMS (Tests of Engineering Aptitude, Mathematics and Science), 62
technical college, 32, 34, 44, 46
technical skills, 22
Technology Accreditation Commission, 38
Technology Student Association (TSA), 53, 61–62
terminology, 28–31
Tests of Engineering Aptitude, Mathematics and Science (TEAMS), 62
thermal collectors, 13
Toll, Micah, 65
tools, 52
tours, 54–55, 58
tracking array, 31
TSA (Technology Student Association), 53, 61–62

U
unions, 25
university, 36, 38
US Department of Energy, 41, 47, 59, 62–63, 74
US Department of Labor (USDL)
    discussion, 9, 67, 69
    salaries, 24–26
US Energy Information Administration, 14, 18, 63
Usher, Bruce, 74
US military
    discussion, 9, 26, 39, 44, 69
    education, 40–41
US News & World Report, 23

V
Vermont Technical College, 46–47
veterans, 9, 41

W
Walmart, 69
Wilson, Kyle, 65
Wind and Solar Power Systems (Patel & Beik), 74
wind power
    discussion, 12, 18, 29–30, 46
    future of, 69, 71
    military, 40
wind power technicians, 67
Wind Solar Alliance, 63–64, 68
women, 10
Women of Renewable Industries and Sustainable Energy (WRISE), 54, 63
WorldSkills International, 61

Y
YouTube, 51–52

CREDITS

Cover: © BAIVECTOR/Shutterstock; © Kampan/Shutterstock; © Waraphorn Aphai/Shutterstock; © Frame Stock Footage/Shutterstock; © only_kim/Shutterstock
6: yuttana Contributor Studio, Shutterstock
11: S.Phoophinyo, Shutterstock
12: Julie Holland, US Department of Agriculture
14: US Department of Energy
15: Monthira, Shutterstock
16: US Department of Energy
19: anatoliy gleb, Shutterstock
20: Ju PhotoStocker, Shutterstock
21: Kampan, Shutterstock
22: US Navy
24: zstock, Shutterstock
32: Gorodenkoff, Shutterstock
34: Oksana Klymenko, Shutterstock
35: pan demin, Shutterstock
37: Soonthorn Wongsaita, Shutterstock
38: Airman 1st Class Jason Couillard, US Air Force
40: Mass Communication Specialist 2nd Class Jon Husman, US Navy
41: US Department of Energy
42: fizkes, Shutterstock
50: Stefano Paltera, US Department of Energy
52: rightclickstudios, Shutterstock
53: StudioFI, Shutterstock
54: Coleman photographer, Shutterstock
55: myphotobank.com.au, Shutterstock
56: VLADJ55, Shutterstock
60: US Army
62: Laurie Loweecey, US Department of Energy
66: Julie Holland, US Department of Agriculture
68: ND700, Shutterstock
70: Heather Wharram, Shutterstock

AUTHOR'S BIOGRAPHY

Andrew Morkes is the founder and editorial director of College & Career Press in Chicago, Illinois. He has written about college- and career-related topics for more than 25 years. Andrew is the author of more than 50 books about college planning and careers, including many titles in the Vault Career Guides series (including *Law, Pharmaceuticals and Biotechnology,* and *Information Technology);* Mason Crest's Careers in the Building Trades and Cool Careers in Science series; *College Spotlight* newsletter, the *CAM Report* career newsletter; and *They Teach That in College!?: A Resource Guide to More Than 100 Interesting College Majors,* which was selected as one of the best books of the year by the library journal *Voice of Youth Advocates.* He is also the author and publisher of "The Morkes Report: College and Career Planning Trends" blog. Andrew is a member of the parent advisory board at his son's school. He is also the author of *Nature in Chicagoland: More Than 120 Fantastic Nature Destinations That You Must Visit.* Articles about Andrew's work have appeared in the *Chicago Tribune,* the *Chicago Sun-Times, Practical Homeschooling,* and other publications.